Where's the Key to the Safe?

WORKBOOK

PAM BAKER *and*
CAMERON ZABKO, CFP®

Where's the Key to the Safe?

WORKBOOK

HOW *to* AVOID PROBATE PITFALLS *and* MAXIMIZE FAMILY FINANCES

www.lastinglegacyconsulting.com

Paperback: 979-8-9918570-4-8

Printed in: Georgia, United States

Ordering Information:
Special discounts are available on quantity purchases by corporations, associations, and others. For details, contact contact@lastinglegacyconsulting.com

Table of Contents

Intro

This workbook was designed to accompany the book *Where's The Key to the Safe? How to Avoid Probate Pitfalls and Maximize Family Finances*. If you do not own this book, I suggest you order a copy. While this workbook will be useful to you, it will make much more sense if you complete the following exercises while reading the corresponding chapters in the book. If you are completing this workbook in conjunction with reading the book, we suggest using the workbook to take notes throughout each chapter then completing the exercises once you have read through the entire chapter. Because the first chapter of the book is an introduction to *why* the book was created, it has been omitted from this workbook. This workbook begins in conjunction with the second chapter of the book.

Our hope is that after reading the book and completing this workbook that you have all the firepower at your disposal to identify gaps in your or your loved one's current plan, make necessary changes, communicate the plan effectively to those involved, and have the confidence to speak to financial and legal professionals on how to execute the plan if necessary. Just as in the book, this workbook is not designed to provide tax, financial, or legal advice. It is simply a tool to organize your estate plan into an efficient and communicable set of documents.

Throughout this workbook we have put an asterisk next to important information to include in your estate planning organizer referenced in the book. An estate planning organizer can be as formal or informal as you want to make it. In essence it a collection of your important documents, final wishes, and information you wish for your loved ones to know. A good estate planning organizer will allow your executor, spouse, or loved to read through it and easily find accounts and answers to questions they have regarding your estate.

We have provided the same glossary at the end of this workbook that is provided at the end of the book. If you are wondering what a term means while reading, please feel free to use either glossary. If you get stuck, please email contact@lastinglegacyconsulting.com. We are more than happy to answer questions or point you in a helpful direction.

CHAPTER 2

The Bare Minimum

Please select yes or no and write in the appropriate answers as they relate to you or the person you are helping to draft an estate plan for.

Wills

1. Do you have a will? (YES/NO)
2. Do you have access to a digital and original signed copy of your will? (YES/NO)
3. *Where is it located?
4. Do you live in the same state as you did when this will was drafted or last amended? (YES/NO)
5. When was the will drafted or last amended?
6. When was the last time you reviewed the will for inaccuracies?
7. Has there been a death, divorce, remarriage, falling out, or birth that is not reflected in your current will? (YES/NO)
8. Do you understand how your assets will be passed to your heirs based on your current will? (YES/NO)
9. Are you comfortable with your current will as written? (YES/NO)

If you answered no to any of these questions, then it is time to read through your current will and decide if it needs to be updated. If you are unsure, then you should speak with an estate planning attorney about your concerns. If you do not have the funds to consult with an estate planning attorney, then creating new documents with an online service may be your best bet.

Trusts

1. Do you have minor children or an adult child that is unable to care for his or herself? (YES/NO)
2. Do you have concerns that your heirs may need restrictions as to not blow through their inheritance or use it in ways you do not approve of? (YES/NO)
3. Is your estate greater than $5,000,000 (single) or $10,000,000 (married)? (YES/NO)
4. Do you have family members that you would like to guarantee do not receive any of your assets upon your passing? (YES/NO)
5. Are any of your heirs married to a person that you would like to cut out of your inheritance in the event your heir gets divorced or dies? (YES/NO)

6. Would you like to maintain anonymity for your heirs so as to not alert the public about their recent inheritance? (YES/NO)
7. Are you remarried? (YES/NO) If NO, skip questions 8–11.
8. Do you have children from a previous marriage that you would like to leave an inheritance to? (YES/NO)
9. After you pass, would your current spouse be dependent on any or all of your assets to maintain the same quality of life? (YES/NO)
10. Would you like to continue providing assistance to your current spouse after you pass? (YES/NO)
11. Would you like to have your assets pass to your kids, heirs, or charity upon your surviving spouse's passing? (YES/NO)

If you answered YES to any of the questions above, you may need a trust. Trusts provide an additional layer of security that a simple will cannot. A financial advisor is a great starting point to determine if a trust is necessary. Sometimes your goals can be accomplished far less expensively by changing beneficiary designations and updating your will than by creating a trust.

12. Does your estate plan include a trust? (YES/NO) If NO, skip the next section: *Basics.*
13. Do you have access to a digital and original signed copy of your trust? (YES/NO)
14. *Where is it located?
15. Is the trust revocable or irrevocable?
16. When was the trust drafted or last amended?
17. When was the last time you reviewed the trust for inaccuracies?
18. Has there been a death, divorce, remarriage, falling out, or birth that is not reflected in your current trust? (YES/NO)
19. Do you understand how your assets will be passed to your heirs based on your current trust? (YES/NO)
20. Are you comfortable with your current trust as written? (YES/NO)

If you cannot answer the questions in the above section or do not understand the purpose of your current trust, then I implore you to consult with an estate planning attorney to determine if your trust is fulfilling your estate planning goals or if it needs to be redrafted or revoked.

Basics

1. *My medical power of attorney agent is:
2. *My medical power of attorney agent also has a HIPPA release form to access my medical records. (YES/NO)
3. *My financial power of attorney is:
4. Do my agent(s) know where the original documents or copies are in the event of an emergency. (YES/NO)
5. *Where are these documents located?
6. *The executor/executrix of my estate is:
7. *The guardian(s) for ________________________(kids/pets names) is/are ________________.
8. I have discussed the roles and responsibilities of each of the above with the named person. (YES/NO)

If you are stuck trying to fill the roles above, try asking yourself the questions below. These are very vital roles to fill. Remember you can always change these documents in the future to swap out these "players" on your "team."

1. Who do I admire for their financial knowledge and/or decisions?
2. Who do I think knows me the best and would respect my final wishes?
3. Who would take the best care of my kids or pets?
4. Who would respect my medical wishes in the event I cannot communicate them?

*In the event you are incapacitated, provide the following medical information for your medical POA:

Doctor(s) and Contact Information:	Medications, Times Taken/ Needed, and Location:	Medical History:

*Assets

For the below table, record the location (bank, custodian, company, etc.) beneficiaries, and last four digits of the account number for all of your assets. You do not need to put the current value of the accounts unless if helps you with the exercise.

Type of Account	Location	Beneficiaries
Retirement Accounts • IRA • Roth IRA • 401k/ 403b		

Bank Accounts • Checking • Savings • High-Yield or Online • CD's or MMKT		
Taxable Accounts • Taxable Brokerage Accounts • TOD • JTWROS		
Annuities • Taxable Annuities • IRA/Retirement Annuities		

Tangible Items • Precious Metals • Safety Deposit Box • Other		

Reflective Questions

1. Do my beneficiary designations align with my will or trust?
2. Does my estate plan need an inspection, a tune up, or a full rebuild?
3. Can I confidently explain my estate plan and how assets will move to my heirs?
4. Have I talked to all the people involved so they are aware of their roles in the event of an emergency?

CHAPTER 3

Teamwork Makes the Dream Work—Building Your Professional Team

Please select yes or no and write in the appropriate answers as they relate to you or the person you are helping to draft an estate plan for.

*Contact info:

My current financial advisor is:

Their contact information is:

My current CPA is:

Their contact information is:

My current estate planning attorney is:

Their contact information is:

Auditing your Team and Relationship Review

1. Do you currently work with a financial advisor? (YES/NO) If NO, are you holding yourself to the same standards as you would a professional? (YES/NO)
2. Would you recommend your current advisor to a family member? (YES/NO)
3. Is your advisor a fiduciary? (YES/NO)
4. Does your advisor take the time to educate you on why they are making their choices or recommendations regarding your portfolio or financial plan? (YES/NO)
5. Does your advisor offer comprehensive financial planning including not just a performance review and retirement projections but also tax mitigation strategies, retirement and large expense distribution planning, Social Security maximization strategies, life, disability, and long-term care insurance gap analysis, education planning, and how all this ties into your estate plan? (YES/NO)
6. Does your advisor meet with your CPA or other members of your legal or tax team to ensure legal and tax strategies are implemented correctly? (YES/NO)
7. Do you trust your current advisor (YES/NO)?
8. Would you hire your current advisor again knowing what you know now? (YES/NO)

If you answered NO to any of these questions, then you have some soul searching to do. What is your advisor currently not doing that would improve your relationship? Can this relationship be repaired by communicating your needs or is this relationship beyond repair? Do not stay with your current advisor strictly out of loyalty.

You need to do what is best for you and your family's wealth. The same goes for CPA relationships. If you are currently working with a tax preparer and would rather be working with a tax planner, then you need to communicate these needs with your current CPA or find a new CPA to work with.

Reflective Questions

1. Do I understand how my current estate plan satisfies my financial, charitable, or legacy goals?
2. Do I understand how my tax, retirement, financial, and estate plan relate and complement each other?
3. Do I understand what services my financial, legal, and tax team provides? Am I utilizing them correctly? Do they fulfill my needs?

CHAPTER 4

Risky Business—The Ins and Outs of P&C Insurance

It is important to shop your property and casualty insurance every three to five years to ensure you are still receiving competitive premium rates. Insurance companies know that humans become complacent. They will increase your rates disproportionately, betting on the fact that you are too lazy to research what other options you have. Even if you are not planning on changing insurance carriers, it is still a good idea to tell your current agent that you are shopping around to see if they will give you a better rate. In any scenario, make sure you are getting an apples-to-apples comparison for your current policies and not a quote for policies with inferior coverage.

P&C Review

Please select yes or no and write in the appropriate answers as they relate to you or the person you are helping to draft an estate plan for.

AUTO

1. When was the last time you shopped your home, auto, and umbrella policies? If your answer was more than five years ago, then it is time to start shopping around.
2. What are your current liability limits for your auto policy?
3. Referring to the car accident examples in chapter four of the book, are you comfortable with your current limits? (YES/NO)
4. Do you have comprehensive coverage for your vehicle? (YES/NO)
5. Do you have collision coverage for your vehicle? (YES/NO)
6. If you said NO to 4 or 5, are you able to self-insure the cost of replacing your vehicle if it is totaled? (YES/NO)
7. Do you have uninsured/underinsured motorist coverage? (YES/NO)
8. What are the limits for the policy?
9. Are you comfortable with this protection? (YES/NO)
10. What is your premium?
11. Compared to other quotes you received recently, does this premium seem fair? (YES/NO)
12. What are your deductibles?
13. Can you afford to pay your current deductibles out of pocket? (YES/NO)
14. Can you afford to increase your deductibles and pay more out of pocket for an accident to reduce your premiums? (YES/NO)

HOME

1. What form of homeowner's policy do you have for your home?
2. Have you increased the protected value in the last three to five years? (YES/NO) If NO, contact your agent and discuss the protected value of your home under your current policy. Most homes have appreciated in value tremendously in recent years and building prices have skyrocketed. This could leave you underinsured in the event of a total loss of your home.
3. Are you comfortable with your current coverage? (YES/NO)
4. Do you have any valuables or concerns you need to discuss with your agent? (YES/NO)
5. What is your premium?
6. Compared to other quotes you received recently, does this premium seem fair? (YES/NO)
7. What is your deductible?
8. Can you afford to pay your current deductibles out of pocket? (YES/NO)
9. Can you afford to increase your deductibles and pay more out of pocket for an accident to reduce your premiums? (YES/NO)

UMBRELLA

1. Do you have an umbrella liability policy? (YES/NO)
2. Is your net worth over $1M? (YES/NO)
3. If you answered NO to question 1 and YES to question 2 then you should discuss adding an umbrella policy with your agent.
4. Have you updated the coverage amount of your umbrella policy in proportion to your net worth? (YES/NO) If NO, contact your agent and discuss your options for increasing your umbrella policy to protect more of your assets. The coverage is very affordable and provides a lot of protection for the price.
5. What is your premium?
6. Compared to other quotes you received recently, does this premium seem fair? (YES/NO)

Reflective Questions

1. Do I understand what my current P&C policies cover? Am I adequately protected against a total loss of my home or a major car accident?
2. When was the last time I shopped for my P&C coverage? Am I paying a fair premium for the coverage provided?
3. Are there specific concerns I have that I need to ask my P&C agent about to verify I am covered?

CHAPTER 5

From Crutches to Coffins—Disability and Life Insurance

Please select yes or no and write in the appropriate answers as they relate to you or the person you are helping to draft an estate plan for.

Disability Insurance

1. Are you retired or able to comfortably retire tomorrow? (YES/NO) If YES, skip to the section: *Life Insurance.*
2. Do you have a risky job or medical issues/illnesses that may lead to a disability? (YES/NO)
3. Could you sustain a 3-month interruption to your paycheck? (YES/NO)
4. Do you have a short-term disability insurance policy? (YES/NO)

If you answered YES to question 2 or NO to questions 1, 3, or 4, then you should look into obtaining a short-term disability policy. The most cost-effective and easiest way to get coverage is typically a group policy through your employer. If your employer does not offer coverage, then you will need to purchase a private policy. Make sure you weigh the pros and cons of a short-term policy. Disability policies can be expensive and if you have the capital to sustain a 7–90-day disruption to your cashflow then you may not need a short-term disability policy.

1. If you lost your ability to work tomorrow, would your family be able to maintain their same standard of living without your paycheck? (YES/NO)
2. If you lost your ability to work tomorrow, would your current assets support you through the rest of your life? (YES/NO)
3. Do you have a long-term disability insurance policy? (YES/NO)

If you answered NO to either question 5 or 6 and also NO to question 7, then you may need to purchase a long-term disability policy. Like a short-term policy, the easiest and most cost-effective way to get long-term disability insurance is through your employer. The critical option you need to consider is whether the policy is *any* or *own* occupation protection. You can read more about the differences in chapter 5 of the book, but to summarize, own occupation tends to provide better coverage at a higher price.

Accident Indemnity and Illness Insurance

These insurance types are usually purchased as part of a group policy through your employer. Analyze your pay-stub and benefits package to identify what policies are available to you and which ones you are currently paying for. If you have limited liquidity (cash on hand), then it may make sense to purchase or continue paying for these types of policies. If you have plenty of cash on hand to cover a hospital stay or not be reimbursed for cancer treatments, then the premiums you are paying may better serve you by being diverted to investments.

In the space below, fill in the information relating to your current disability policies:

**Include in Estate Planning Organizer*

Company and Policy Number	Elimination and Benefit Period	Benefit Amount
Short Term:		
Long Term:		
Accident and Sickness:	N/A	Qualifying Incident: Benefit Amount:

Life Insurance

1. Do you have a risky job or a family history of medical issues/illnesses that may lead to an early death? (YES/NO)
2. Would someone in your life be financially burdened if you passed away? (YES/NO)
3. If you passed away tomorrow, would your family be able to maintain their same standard of living without your paycheck, pension, or Social Security income? (YES/NO/UNSURE)
4. Do you have a life insurance policy? (YES/NO)

If you answered YES to questions 1 and 2 and NO or UNSURE to questions 3 and 4, then it is recommended that you speak to a financial or insurance professional to determine if a life insurance policy is appropriate for your situation.

5. Is this policy's benefit large enough to fill the gap left behind after your passing? (YES/NO/UNSURE)
6. Is this policy too large for your current needs? (YES/NO/UNSURE)
7. Can you cancel your life insurance policy? (YES/NO/UNSURE)

If you answered NO or UNSURE to question 5 and YES or UNSURE to questions 6 and 7, then we recommend that you speak to a financial or insurance professional to determine if you are over- or under-insured. **Do not** cancel your policy until you determine if you are adequately insured.

In the spaces below, fill in the information relating to your current life insurance policies:

**Include in Estate Planning Organizer*

Death Benefit	Company and Policy Number	Beneficiaries
Term Life (include purchase date and term length):		
Whole Life:		
Variable Life:		
Group (Work)		

Reflective Questions

1. How would my or my family's cash flow be impacted if I became disabled and lost 20%–60% of my income tomorrow?
2. Is there anyone financially dependent on my ability to earn an income? How would they survive if I passed away unexpectedly?
3. What is my current need for life and disability insurance? Do I still need the life and/or disability policies I purchased in the past?

CHAPTER 6

Passwords, Financials, and Deeds, Oh My!

Please select yes or no and write in the appropriate answers as they relate to you or the person you are helping to draft an estate plan for.

1. Do you have your passwords stored in a way that others will be able to access them? (YES/NO)

*If you are using a password manager, write the website, username, and password in the space below:

Website Address	Username	Password

*In the space below, record common four and six digit pins you use (Phone, Bank, Etc.):

Common Four Digit Pins.	Common Six Digit Pins.

*For the list of common security questions below, record your answers in the space provided:

- What is your mother's maiden name?
- What was your first job?
- What is the name of your favorite pet?
- What high school did you attend? What was their mascot?
- What was the name of your elementary school?
- What was the make of your first car?
- What was your favorite food as a child?
- Where did you meet your spouse?
- What year was your father and mother born?
- What street did you grow up on?

2. Do you know where the titles are for your personal property (real estate, cars, boats)? (YES/NO)
3. *Where are these documents located?
4. Do you have them titled in both you and your spouse's names? (YES/NO)

5. *Do you have a list of trusted, reliable companies (mechanic, plumber, electrician, handyman, dry cleaners) recorded somewhere? (YES/NO)
6. *Do you have a list of your clubs and organizations that you belong to or volunteer with? (YES/NO)
7. *Do you have a list of your social media accounts? (YES/NO)
8. *Have you written down your final wishes for your end-of-life ceremony? (YES/NO)
9. Have you overly communicated your estate plan to the necessary players and/or heirs? (YES/NO)
10. Is your financial footprint as streamlined as possible to it is easy for your heirs to access their inheritance and close out your estate? (YES/NO)
11. *Do you have any old accounts or assets that will be lost or difficult to find after you pass? (YES/NO)

If you answered NO to any of the these questions, then you have some work to do. It is vital for your loved ones and executor to be aware of your final wishes, locations of important documents and accounts, and to simplify your financial footprint as much as possible. This will also make your life easier and more organized as well.

Estate Planning Organizer

Do you have an estate planning organizer? (YES/NO)

Throughout this workbook we have put an asterisk next to important information to include in your estate planning organizer. An estate planning organizer can be as formal or informal as you want to make it. In essence it is a collection of your important documents, final wishes, and information you wish for your loved ones to know. A good estate planning organizer will allow your executor, spouse, or loved one to read through it and easily find accounts and answers to questions they have regarding your estate. Once completed, this workbook can serve as a great basis for your estate planning organizer! Below is an additional list of items to include:

1. Who to contact at time of death and their contact info (family, friends, doctors, professionals, etc.).
2. Original copies of your will and other estate planning documents or the location of where to find them.
3. A list of where important valuables, documents, passports are kept.
4. A list of keys and their locations for your home, car, storage unit, boat, lawnmower, ATV, golfcart, etc. It is recommended that you make copies, label, and store these copies in one place (like your safe).
5. A Letter to your loved ones explaining anything you feel is important including your final wishes, why your estate plan is set up the way it is, specific items you want to go to individuals, and any other details you find meaningful.

Reflective Questions

1. Is my financial footprint as streamlined as possible, so it is easy for my heirs to access their inheritance and close out my estate?
2. What do I want in terms of an end-of-life ceremony?
3. Do I have any old accounts or assets that will be lost or difficult to find after my passing?

CHAPTER 7

Designing Your Cash Flow Like a Pro

Please select yes or no and write in the appropriate answers as they relate to you or the person you are helping to draft an estate plan for.

1. Do you have a good understanding of what you are spending each month on living expenses? (YES/NO)
2. Do you have an accurate account of your cashflow (what assets come in and leave your household each month)? (YES/NO)

If you answered NO to the first two questions you will want to complete the cashflow exercise explained in chapter 7 of the book. Having a cashflow report will help you to identify waste and channel excess spending toward debt, goals, vacation, or whatever else is important to you. We find that dissecting your cashflow works better for correcting wasteful spending than budgeting long term.

3. Do you have an emergency fund for unexpected expenses to avoid being forced to use debt to cover emergencies? (YES/NO)
4. Do you have a high-yield savings account that you actively transfer money to each month? (YES/NO)
5. Are you holding too much cash? (YES/NO/UNSURE)

If you answered NO or UNSURE to questions 3–5 then you will want to take a minute an complete the Liquidity Ladder exercise outlined in chapter 7 of the book. This exercise will help you set a target for the amount of cash you need on hand. If you are holding too little cash currently, you now have a savings goal. If you are holding too much cash currently then you can look for ways to deploy this excess capital into investments, home renovations, or other large purchases or goals.

6. Do you have an effective strategy in place to pay off current debt? (YES/NO/UNSURE)
7. Do you have your bills and credit cards set up on auto-pay? (YES/NO)

If you are struggling to pay off debt the best place to start is with the cashflow exercise. Once you identify wasteful spending, direct that money toward debt using the snowball method or by paying off your highest interest debt first. Setting up auto-pay will ensure your credit score is not impacted because you forgot to pay your bills.

In the space below, fill in the information relating to your current debt. This exercise will help you to identify where to make extra debt payments.

Lender	Interest Rate	Remaining Term	Balance	Current Monthly Payment
Credit Cards:		N/A		
Other Debt:				

If you've never had to manage the household financial, legal, or tax matters, have you discussed the following with your spouse or partner? These are also beneficial topics for your executor to understand.

1. *Where are the estate planning documents located? How do I access them (where's the key to the safe)?
2. *How do I pay the bills? Which bills are on autopay and which bills need to be paid manually?
3. *Is there life insurance in place? (YES/NO) If YES, where are the documents and who do I contact to claim it?
4. *Is the emergency fund in a joint bank account, or will I lose access to that account if you pass away? (YES/NO)
5. Are the credit cards joint, or will I lose access to that account if you pass away? (YES/NO)
6. *Where are all the investment accounts, and how or who do I contact to access them? Compile a net worth statement and a list of logins and passwords with instructions on accessing them to avoid money getting lost in the ether.
7. How will I access medical insurance? This is especially important if your spouse's employer provides medical insurance.

Chapter 7 is one of, if not the most, important chapters for everyone reading this book. It is especially important if you are in a relationship in which your spouse or partner handles all the financial, legal, and tax matters. If your person passes away and you are clueless as to how to run the household's finances, you will be in the very difficult position of having to learn all this new information while grieving your loss. Important to-do's will slip through the cracks and you may fall behind on bills, lose access to liquidity, go into debt, or worse. This will culminate in you feeling much more overwhelmed than you need to be in your time of grief and leave you questioning your confidence in your financial future. Take it from Pam and do your homework ahead of time.

Reflective Questions

1. Will I or a financial dependent have access to liquidity in the event my spouse or I passes away or is incapacitated?
2. Do I know how much money I need every month to sustain my current standard of living?
3. Do I understand how and when bills and monthly expenses are paid?
4. Am I comfortable with my current emergency savings? Am I holding too much cash?

CHAPTER 8

Life After Death

Most of this chapter will only apply once a person is deceased. There are, however, tasks you can do before the passing of your loved one to make the process easier for yourself in the future. You can also help your loved one complete these tasks in the event you predecease them. The questions below are designed to help in this process. The death of a loved one is never easy, but completing these tasks ahead of time will ensure a smoother transition.

Please select yes or no and write in the appropriate answers as they relate to you or the person you are helping to draft an estate plan for.

Pre-Death

1. Is my credit frozen with the three major credit bureaus? (YES/NO/UNSURE)
2. Have you chosen your wingman to help you navigate life after the death of your loved one? (YES/NO)
3. Do you have an efficient tax and distribution plan in place to combat the widow tax? (YES/NO)
4. Do you understand how your expenses will or will not change if your spouse predeceases you? (YES/NO)
5. Have you identified the benefits provided by your and your loved one's current or former employer(s) that you or they will be entitled to in the event of your or their passing? (YES/NO)

If you answered NO to any of these questions, then you have some homework to do. A financial planner will be able to help you research questions 3–5.

Post-Death

The following list are items to do soon after the passing of a loved one. If these do not apply to you currently, then save this list for future use:

1. Have you ordered death certificates and know where to pick them up? (YES/NO)
2. Have you contacted Social Security regarding surviving spouse and dependent children benefits? (YES/NO)
3. Have you contacted your professional team? (YES/NO)
4. Have you contacted the deceased's employer? (YES/NO)
5. If retired, have you contacted the pension company to see if you qualify for surviving spousal benefits? (YES/NO)
6. Have you frozen the deceased's credit cards and bank accounts to avoid identity fraud? (YES/NO)

7. Have you scheduled a credit freeze with the three major credit bureaus on the deceased's credit to prevent criminals from applying for loans in their name? (YES/NO)
8. Have you submitted death claims and returned the necessary signed paperwork so assets can be transferred to the correct beneficiaries? (YES/NO)
9. If there is a large or complicated estate involved, do you have an accurate assessment of its value on the date of death? (YES/NO)
10. Have you contacted an estate planning attorney to begin the probate process? (YES/NO)

Reflective Questions

1. When reading through all the work someone will need to do for my estate, are there things I can do today to make their job easier later?
2. What are my tax and distribution plans in the event my spouse dies to combat the widow tax?
3. How will my expenses change if my spouse predeceases me?

CHAPTER 9

Taxes and the ABCs of RMDs

This is a relatively short chapter when it comes to the workbook, but the information covered in chapter 9 is invaluable. A tax-efficient estate plan does not have to be complicated. Often times it can be solved by adjusting the beneficiaries on your investment accounts to give different percentages of each account to your heirs. Required minimum distributions are a little more challenging to combat, but working with a good financial and tax planner could save you and your heirs thousands of dollars in unnecessary tax payments down the road. It can be difficult to see the value of going this extra mile, but I can guarantee it is worth it to ensure your heirs are receiving the maximum inheritance possible.

Please select yes or no and write in the appropriate answers as they relate to you or the person you are helping to draft an estate plan for.

1. Are you aware of required minimum distribution rules for your heirs on tax-deferred accounts like traditional IRAs? (YES/NO)
2. Have you talked to a professional regarding Roth conversions or other tax mitigation strategies for your tax-deferred accounts? (YES/NO)
3. Is your estate plan designed to mitigate taxes for your beneficiaries? (YES/NO/UNSURE)
4. *Do you have beneficiary, TOD, and POD designations on all of your accounts? (YES/NO/UNSURE)

If you answered NO or UNSURE to any of these questions, then it may be time to talk to a financial or tax planner. These strategies such as Roth conversions can get complicated and we do not advise you try to enact them without speaking with a professional.

5. Is your net worth greater than $5,000,000 (single) or $10,000,000 (married)? (YES/NO)
6. If YES, are you working with a tax planner and/or financial advisor to reduce your possible estate tax down the road? (YES/NO)

If your net worth exceeds the thresholds discussed above, you should absolutely work with a professional team to mitigate both your current taxes and potential future estate taxes owed by your heirs.

Reflective Questions

1. Do I have a strategy to mitigate taxes during my lifetime?
2. Do I have a strategy to reduce the taxes my heirs pay for the assets they will inherit?
3. Is there a more tax-efficient way to pass my assets to the next generation or charity?
4. Do I have beneficiary, TOD, and POD designations on all my accounts?

CHAPTER 10

Ensuring Your Business Lives on After You're Gone

Estate planning for business owners can be especially complicated. It is important not to be intimidated by the process and do nothing. Inaction could lead to your business faltering in the event you are unable to continue running it. If your loved ones are dependent on the revenue generated by or the future sale of the business to maintain their current lifestyle, then you need to do the work today to protect your and their future income source.

Please select yes or no and write in the appropriate answers as they relate to you or the person you are helping to draft an estate plan for.

1. Have you checked your state's missing property website for assets owed to you or your deceased loved ones? (YES/NO)
2. Are you or your spouse a business owner? (YES/NO) If NO you can skip the rest of this chapter, but please share this book with any business owner in your life!
3. *Do you have a succession or continuity plan in place to protect your employees, family, and customers from the negative impact of your passing? (YES/NO)
4. *Have you identified a possible successor who could run the business in your absence? (YES/NO)
5. Do you have a strategy in place to decouple yourself from your business prior to retirement? (YES/NO)
6. If you are not working day to day in the business, have you established relationships with the key employees? (YES/NO)
7. Have you considered how you will access health insurance if the primary business owner passes away/the business is sold? (YES/NO)
8. Have you considered life insurance as a cost-effective way to provide liquidity for your company following your death or the death of a key employee? (YES/NO)
9. Have you conducted a business valuation to see if selling your business is a viable option to fund your retirement or provide for your family in the event of your death? (YES/NO)
10. Have you considered hiring a business coach to keep you accountable and help you make decisions that will improve the functionality and value of your business? (YES/NO)
11. Have you set up an estate plan for your business? (YES/NO)
12. Do you have a list of companies that you receive payments, such as commission checks and debt payments from? (YES/NO)

If you answered NO to any of these questions, then you have some work to do. This can seem like a daunting task on top of running your business and life's daily requirements, but I promise it is very important. The goal with these to-do's is not to design a business that will run perfectly without you. Rather these plans provide breathing room for your family and employees in the event of your incapacitation to regroup and make decisions on the future of the business without negative impacts on your cashflow or customers.

Reflective Questions

1. What would happen to my business, my employees, my customers, and those who depend on my income if I pass away tomorrow?
2. Is there someone I trust to run my business in my absence?
3. Am I depending on the sale or continuation of my business to fund my retirement or provide enough money for my family in the event of my death?

Glossary

401k: Retirement account offered by an employer that allows employees to defer pre-taxed portions of their paychecks and invest these funds in a preselected lineup of investment vehicles. Some plans offer Roth (post-tax) options as well.

403b: Same concept as a 401k except offered by a non-profit, government agency, school, religious organization, or other public sector entity.

529 Account: Education savings vehicle that allows family members or friends to contribute state-tax differed money for a student's future educational expenses.

Actual Cash Value (ACV): The current value of your assets that an insurance company is responsible for paying you after a claim. ACV tends to be lower than replacement costs because your assets tend to depreciate in value over time.

Advance Medical Directive: Legal document created to convey your wishes for medical intervention and treatment in the event you are incapacitated. This document also names a medical power of attorney.

Annuity: A contract with an insurance company where you promise to give the insurance company a certain amount of money for a specified period of time. In return, the insurance company promises you a certain payout in the future, a set rate of return, or some other guarantees.

Any Occupation: A category of disability insurance that deems you disabled if you are unable to work any occupation. Under an any occupation policy, you will have a harder time proving you are disabled when compared to an own occupation policy.

Assets Under Management (AUM): The assets managed by a financial professional. Fees are usually charged as a percentage of your assets managed by the financial professional.

Beneficiary: A person who is named to inherit tangible or intangible assets from a benefactor.

Beneficiary Designation: The legal naming of a person, charity, or entity to inherit an asset. Usually used for retirement and other investment or insurance accounts.

Bequeathment: Passing of assets to your beneficiaries through a will.

Captive Agent: An insurance agent that only sells policies from a single insurance company.

Cash Value: In a permanent life insurance policy, the cash value is the value that accumulates over time that you can access while you are still alive. This is also the amount returned to you if you cancel the policy.

Cash Flow: The money coming into and leaving your household during a period of time.

CERTIFIED FINANCIAL PLANNER®: A financial planner who has completed the requirements of becoming a CERTIFIED FINANCIAL PLANNER®. Planners with this designation specialize in holistic financial planning instead of just investment advice.

Collision Insurance: Car insurance that pays to repair or replace your vehicle if you cause an accident.

Commission-Based Product: An investment or insurance product that pays the agent or advisor for selling the product rather than compensation tied to the performance of the product.

Comprehensive Coverage: Car insurance that pays to repair or replace your vehicle if something other than a car accident causes damage to your vehicle.

Comprehensive Financial Planning: Also known as holistic financial planning, this process involves looking at all aspects that affect you financially, including but not limited to taxes, planning for retirement, post-retirement distribution planning, disability, debt utilization planning, long-term care, college planning, life insurance needs, and how your investments tie into all these aspects. This contrasts with investment advisors who are tasked with strictly designing an investment portfolio or insurance agents selling you a disability, life, annuity, or long-term care policy.

Cost of Living Adjustment: Also referred to as COLA, this adjustment is most prevalent in pensions, fixed income, or insurance benefits, and increases your benefit based on a set amount each year or the rate of inflation.

Certified Public Accountant (CPA): A tax professional who can help prepare your tax return and/or plan and execute a long-term tax mitigation strategy. CPAs can also work with businesses to help with bookkeeping and keeping entities tax-compliant.

Death Benefit: The amount of money paid out from a life insurance policy in the event the insured passes away under the terms of the contract.

Debt Utilization Planning: A part of the financial planning process that develops a plan to tackle debt, decide when and how to use debt, and ensure you are maximizing the amount of interest flowing into your household and decreasing the amount of interest you are paying out.

Deductible: The amount of money stipulated by your home or auto (or health) insurance policy that you must pay out of pocket before the insurance company will start paying for a claim you file. Usually, your deductible and premiums will have an inverse relationship.

Disability Insurance: Insurance designed to provide you with income in the event you are unable to work because of a disability or illness.

Distribution Planning: A part of the financial planning process that game plans the appropriate sequence and source of funds used to pay for retirement or a large expense to mitigate taxes and market, interest rate, inflation, and other risks.

Do Not Resuscitate (DNR): A legal document outlining the circumstances in which you do or do not want medical intervention to bring you back to life or prevent your death. This document provides guidance to medical power of attorney.

Elimination Period: Similar to a deductible, the elimination period represents the amount of time you must wait before a disability insurance policy will begin paying your benefit after you are deemed disabled.

Employer-Sponsored Retirement Plan: A retirement investment account that is opened and administered by an employer. Commonly, the employer will contribute and/or match employee contributions to the account.

Estate Organizer: A collection of documents and instructions designed to aid your heirs and executors on how to access assets, distribute personal items, and provide guidance on final wishes. These are important items not contained in your will or other legal documents.

Estate Tax: Taxes owed by a person's estate following their death if their total estate's value exceeds the estate tax exemption.

Estate Tax Exemption: The portion of the value of an estate set by the tax code that is shielded from estate tax consequences.

Executor/Executrix: The person in charge of your estate when you pass away. This person will work to have the estate probated, file the appropriate tax return(s), and have your assets sold and/or disseminated to your heirs.

Fee-Based: A compensation method for financial advisors in which most of their compensation is derived from fees generated from financial planning and/or investment management, but they still sell commission-based products or investments.

Fee-Only: A compensation method for financial advisors in which all their compensation is derived from fees generated from financial planning and/or investment management. They do not sell commission-based products or investments.

Fiduciary Standard: A standard a financial advisor is held to in which they must act in the absolute best interest of their client.

Financial Advisor: A professional providing financial advice above and beyond just investment advice or portfolio management.

Financial Power of Attorney: A person named to take care of your finances and have access to your financial accounts in the event you are incapacitated.

Guardian: A person named to take care of your child(ren) and/or pet(s) in the event of your death.

Generation-Skipping Transfer Tax: A tax introduced in the '70s to deter wealthy individuals from gifting assets to a person one or more generations younger than them to avoid having their true heirs pay estate taxes.

Hazard: A danger or factor that increases the likelihood that a peril (damage) occurs.

Heir: Someone who is named to receive your property after you pass away.

Home Equity Line of Credit (HELOC): A loan collateralized by the equity you have in your home. Similar to a mortgage, but typically at a higher and variable interest rate.

HIPAA Release Form: A legal document providing the person you name access to your medical records.

Homeowners Insurance: Property and casualty insurance purchased to protect your home and/or personal property as well as potentially provide you protection in the event that someone is injured on your property.

Health Savings Account (HSA): A tax-differed investment account that can be used to pay for qualified medical expenses tax-free.

Illiquid: An adjective used to describe an asset that is not easily converted to cash. Examples include real estate, art, collectibles, and some investment vehicles.

Incapacitation: If you are unable to make decisions for yourself because of a mental or physical debilitation.

Independent Agent: An insurance agent that is able to sell policies from multiple insurance companies.

Investment Manager/Advisor: A financial professional who provides investment advice and/or portfolio management and design.

Individual Retirement Account (IRA): A tax-differed investment vehicle with a limited contribution limit and age-based withdrawal rules. You can roll a tax-differed employer-sponsored retirement plan into an IRA.

Joint Tenancy with Rights of Survivorship (JTWROS): A legal designation that can be added to an asset in which two or more people share equal ownership of the asset. After an owner passes away, their share of the asset is divided between the surviving owner(s).

Key Person Insurance: A life insurance policy purchased by a company on the life of an individual that is vital to the operation or value of the business. In the event of this individual's death, the business received a death benefit to provide liquidity to the business.

Liability Insurance: The portion of auto insurance that covers your damages to others if you cause a car accident.

Life Insurance: Insurance designed to provide a payout upon the death of the insured to help cover expenses or replace future unearned income.

Limit: The maximum amount an insurance company will pay for a property and causality insurance claim.

Liquidity: Liquid assets or free cash flow that can be used to cover expenses or be diverted to investing or saving.

Limited Liability Corporation (LLC): A legal entity registered with a state government that establishes a legal barrier between a business and its owner(s).

Long-Term Disability: A disability event typically lasting longer than 90 days or is permanent.

Own Occupation: A category of disability insurance that deems you disabled if you are unable to continue your current occupation at the same level as you were prior to the disability.

Partnership: A business with more than one owner but has not established a legal entity. There is no legal distinction between the owners and the business.

Pension: A retirement benefit typically seen only in the public sector nowadays that provides an income stream for a certain period of time or until death are a person stops working.

Per Capita: Meaning "by heads" in Latin, in the event a beneficiary passes away and the account owner also passes away without updating their beneficiaries, this designation redistributes assets amongst the surviving beneficiaries rather than the original beneficiary's heirs.

Per Stirpes: Meaning "by roots" in Latin and the opposite of Per Capita, this designation has assets flow to a deceased beneficiary's heirs instead of being redistributed amongst the surviving beneficiaries.

Peril: In insurance, a peril is something that causes damage to you or your property. A hazard increases the likelihood of a peril. Fire would be a peril whereas your chimney being clogged would be a hazard that would increase the likelihood of a housefire.

Permanent Life Insurance: Life insurance that does not end after a certain amount of time as long as the premiums are paid.

Personal Injury: A component of car insurance that provides you a benefit to cover medical expenses and lost wages regardless of whether you are at fault for a car accident or not. Personal injury covers you as the premium payer, whereas bodily injury covers others if you caused the accident.

Premium: The money paid to an insurance company in exchange for the protection provided by the policy you are paying for.

Probate: The legal process of passing the assets of a deceased person to their heirs and paying any necessary debts.

Property and Casualty Insurance: Insurance that protects your assets from damage or theft as well as protects you from financial liability in the event you injure someone else or damage their property.

Renters' Insurance: A property and casualty policy that protects renters' personal property from damage or theft of their belongings as well as financial liability in the event you injure someone else or damage their property.

Replacement Cost: The amount an insurance company will provide to replace personal property that was damaged. Replacement costs tend to be higher than actual cash value because your assets tend to depreciate in value over time.

Required Minimum Distribution (RMD): The amount of money the IRS dictates you withdraw from your tax-differed investment account each year once you reach a certain age.

Risk: The probability of an event causing loss in which the insurance company will need to pay out a claim.

Roth IRA: A post-tax retirement vehicle with a limited contribution limit. You can roll a post-tax portion of an employer-sponsored retirement plan into a Roth IRA. There are no RMD rules for Roth assets, and withdrawals are tax-free.

Simplified Employee Pension (SEP IRA): A tax-differed investment vehicle usually used by companies with few to no employees that allows the employer (not the employee) to contribute pre-tax money to the account. SEPs have much higher contribution limits than traditional IRAs.

Short-Term Disability: A disability event typically lasting between 7 and 90 days.

SIMPLE IRA: A tax-differed investment vehicle usually used by companies with few employees that require the employer and allows the employee to contribute pre-tax money to the account. SIMPLE IRAs have slightly higher contribution limits than traditional IRAs.

Sole Proprietorship: A business with more than one owner but has not established a legal entity. There is no legal distinction between the owner and the business.

Succession Planning: A continuity or exit plan for business owners in the event they are incapacitated, pass away, or retire so that the business can remain operational.

Suitability Standard: A standard of care that requires a financial professional to recommend a product or provide advice that puts the client in a better position than they are currently, but it does not need to be the absolute best option. A lower standard of care than the fiduciary standard.

Taxable Brokerage Account: An investment account in which you contribute post-tax dollars. There is no tax-free or tax-differed growth. Instead, you pay capital gains taxes at the time you sell the assets in the account as opposed to when the assets are distributed from the account.

Tax-Differed Investment Account: An investment account in which you contribute pre-tax dollars and pay no tax until you distribute the assets out of the account. Assets distributed are taxed at income tax rates, and these accounts are subject to RMD rules. Traditional IRA, 401k, and 403b accounts are taxed differed.

Term Life Insurance: A non-permanent life insurance policy typically sold in increments of 10 years. Term policies are typically the cheapest coverage you can obtain and offer no cash value accumulation. If you outlive the term outlined in the contract, you receive nothing in return for the premiums you paid over the years.

Time Value of Money: The theory that money is worth more to you today than in the future because of your ability to invest or earn interest on that money.

Transfer on Death (TOD) and Payable on Death (POD): A way to add a benefactor to an account that does not have beneficiary designations and avoid the account needing to be probated. Typically used for bank and taxable brokerage accounts.

Trust: The main purpose of a trust is to direct assets to the appropriate benefactor while avoiding probate. Trusts also enable you to add rules or stipulations on when and how benefactors access their inheritance. There are two main types of trusts (Revocable and Irrevocable). The main difference is that you can easily amend a revocable trust while you are still alive, whereas an irrevocable trust becomes its own legal entity upon creation and is difficult to amend. After you pass away, a revocable trust becomes irrevocable.

Umbrella Policy: Part of your property and casualty insurance lineup, your umbrella policy kicks if you cause an injury or property damage that exceeds your home or auto policy limits. It can also provide additional protections and legal counsel benefits.

Uninsured Motorist: A type of auto insurance that protects you in the event you are hit by an uninsured motorist.

Universal Life Insurance: A permanent life insurance product with flexible premiums and possible cash value accumulation. See chapter 4 of the book for the different types of Universal policies.

Whole Life Insurance: A permanent life insurance product with stable premiums and guaranteed cash value accumulation.

Widow Tax: A colloquial term referring to the common occurrence of monthly expenses increasing after losing a spouse and your tax filing status changing to single, resulting in a larger tax liability and increased expenses.

Will: A legal document used to probate your estate and direct your assets to the appropriate benefactor(s) after you pass away.

Workers' Compensation: Insurance paid for by employers that provide benefits to employees in the event they are injured or become ill due to a work-related incident.

www.ingramcontent.com/pod-product-compliance
Lightning Source LLC
LaVergne TN
LVHW080000210926
848481LV00012B/3627